It's me... a Penguin

AF516747

Om KIDZ
An imprint of Om Books International

First Published in 2019 by

Om KIDZ | Om Books International

Corporate & Editorial Office
A-12, Sector 64, Noida 201 301
Uttar Pradesh, India
Phone: +91 120 477 4100
Email: editorial@ombooks.com
Website: www.ombooksinternational.com

Sales Office
107, Ansari Road, Darya Ganj
New Delhi 110 002, India
Phone: +91 11 4000 9000
Email: sales@ombooks.com
Website: www.ombooks.com

© Om Books International 2019

ISBN: 978-93-86410-41-2

Printed in India

10 9 8 7 6 5 4 3 2 1

ALL RIGHTS RESERVED. No part of this book may be reproduced or transmitted in any form by any means, electronic or mechanical, including photocopying and recording, or by any information storage and retrieval system, except as may be expressly permitted in writing by the publisher.

Contents

WHO ARE YOU?

Hello! I am a penguin. I am a flightless bird. Unlike other birds, I have flippers which help me swim.

Flying vs Swimming

Our short wings, densely packed feathers and heavy bodies make it impossible for us to fly. However, we are excellent swimmers.

HOW BIG ARE YOU?

We can be as tiny as the Blue penguin, which is around 35 cm in height, or as tall as the Emperor penguin, which is 115 to 130 cm tall.

The Blue Penguin

The Blue penguin, also known as the little penguin or the fairy penguin, is the smallest in the species. Blue penguins are very tiny and have pale blue or dark grey feathers.

WHERE DO YOU LIVE?

We live in the Southern hemisphere. We are found in and around Australia and New Zealand. Only two species of penguins are found in Antarctica—the Emperor penguin and the Adelie penguin.

CAN YOU SURVIVE IN WARM CLIMATE?

Yes! The Galapagos islands are the warmest habitat of all penguin homes, with a temperature of around 22.8 °C.

Galapagos Penguin

Galapagos penguins can only be found in the Galapagos Archipelago. They are the only penguins found north of the equator. They have special features which help them adjust to the warm climate.

DO YOU HAVE EARS?

The absence of ear flaps gives us a more streamlined shape. These help us swim easily.

Yes. Unlike human ears, our ears are just holes on both sides of the head. Covered by feathers, they are hard to spot.

We have a special ability to hear above and below the water. We can recognise other penguins by their voices. Parent penguins identify their babies through their voices.

DO YOU HAVE SHORT LEGS?

Yes. We have very short legs, which give us a stocky appearance. Our webbed feet help us walk on ice and swim in water.

Our feet don't freeze because when the temperature falls below 0°C, our body increases the circulation of blood to our feet.

Plantigrade Locomotion

Our feet are located much farther behind, than that of other birds. That's why our walk is called **plantigrade**.

Plantigrade - walking on the soles of feet

A new word to learn

WHAT DO YOU EAT?

I love to eat fish, krill, tiny squid, shrimp and other small sea animals. I catch my food through my beak and swallow it whole.

We do not have teeth. However, we have teeth-like barbs on our tongue and on the roof of our mouth. These barbs point backwards and help us to swallow slippery prey.

CAN YOU DRINK SALT WATER?

WHO ALL ARE THERE IN YOUR FAMILY?

We have a normal body temperature of around 37 to 39 °C.

I have cousins across the world. Some of us live in colder regions, while others live in warmer climate.

Rookeries

We like to live in huge colonies called 'rookeries'.

DO YOU LIVE ON LAND OR IN WATER?

We spend about half our lives on land and the other half in the oceans. We can swim underwater at very high speeds which looks to others like we are flying. Some species can even hold their breath for about 20 minutes in water!

HOW FAST CAN YOU SWIM?

Due to our body shape and size, we can swim at a speed of around 15 to 22 miles per hour. We can stay underwater for a long time, longer than any of our fellow avian friends.

HOW DO YOU CAMOUFLAGE YOURSELF?

Our feathers help us camouflage ourselves and this is called **countershading**.

A new word to learn

Countershading - Protective Colouration

Countershading helps penguins blend in with their surroundings and hide from their prey and predators.

HOW DO YOU KEEP YOURSELF WARM IN WINTER?

We have thick skin, and a thick layer of fat called blubber, under our skin which keeps us warm. We often huddle together for warmth.

The layer of air that our dense feathers retain provides almost complete insulation to our body.

DO YOU LAY EGGS?

Yes, we lay eggs, like other birds. Our eggs take 35 to 65 days to hatch. Our babies leave the nest after one month of their birth.

WHAT ARE BABY PENGUINS CALLED?

Baby penguins are called chicks. The mother Emperor penguin lays a single egg and leaves for fishing. It is the father penguin who balances the egg on his feet, covering it with his brood pouch to keep it cozy and warm. The father penguin takes care of the egg, protecting it against icy cold temperatures.

DO YOU INDULGE IN TOBOGGANING?

Yes. We are fun-loving birds and are often seen **tobogganing**. We lie on our bellies and slide through the ice and snow.

WHAT IS A CATASTROPHIC MOLT?

Once a year, penguins go through a process called 'catastrophic molt', when they lose all their feathers at once. It takes them around 2 to 3 weeks to grow new feathers.

A new word to learn

Tobogganing - sliding downhill over snow

ACTIVITY TIME

PAPER PENGUIN

Things You'll Need

- Orange and black foam paper
- Scissors
- Scrapbook
- Googly eyes
- Glue stick

Cut out the penguin's body as well as its wings from black foam paper.

Glue the cut outs on to the penguin's body.

Take a sheet of orange foam paper and trace your handprints on it.

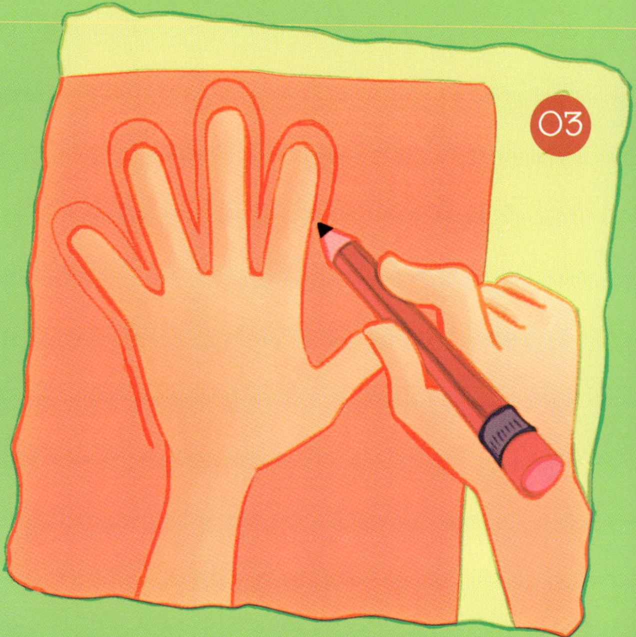

Cut them out to give a round shape.

Glue the cut-outs on to the penguin's body, to make its feet.

Add a colourful scarf (made of scrapbook paper), googly eyes and the beak.

Your penguin is ready!

The penguin is hungry. Help it reach the pond so that it can feast on yummy fish.